HOW TO START YOUR OWN MILLION DOLLAR BUSINESS!

By T.J. Rohleder
Founder of the Direct-Response Network

Also by T.J. Rohleder:

The Black Book of Marketing Secrets (Series)
The Ultimate Wealth-Maker
Ruthless Marketing Attack
Shortcut Secrets to Creating High-Profit Products
Five Secrets That Will Triple Your Profits
24 Simple and Easy Ways to Get Rich Quick
Secrets of the Blue Jeans Millionaire
Four Magical Secrets to Building a Fabulous Fortune
Fast Track to Riches
25 Direct Mail Success Secrets That Can Make You Rich
How to Create a Hot Selling Internet Product in One Day

Introduction

Hello there! This is T.J. Rohleder with the Direct Response Network and M.O.R.E. Inc. and I'm here to tell you "How to Start Your Own Million Dollar Business!" I want to congratulate you for having the wisdom to select and study this book because in so doing you've embarked upon a journey that ninety-nine percent out of a hundred people claim to be interested in making, but never have the gumption to even try. **Right here, in your hands, you're holding valuable secrets that can help you acquire all the money you'll ever need in life** -- if you're willing to put those secrets into action and work hard to make your financial dreams come true.

It's all about taking the necessary steps to convert dreams into reality, a process most people just don't really believe, deep in their hearts, can ever happen. Sure, a lot of people want to make money; they dream of making millions of dollars, but they just don't know how to go about it and don't believe it can really happen to them. **Well, right here, today, I'm going to show you the exact strategies you need to adopt in order to start and run your own million dollar business.**

So who am I to make that kind of claim? Who am I to tell you how to make millions of dollars? Very simply, I'm someone who's actually done all the things I'll be telling you about. I started on the ground floor (or actually, a little below it) 20 years ago with $300 in my pocket and with the help of my wife and business associates -- and a lot of determination and elbow grease -- I've built that start-up money into a business that's grossed over $110 million so far. So I know just what I'm talking about and this publication is my way of passing this hard-earned knowledge on to you. **In the following pages, I'll answer a dozen specific questions that customers ask me every day about how to build a successful business**, using examples from my own experience and that of my closest business associates -- including my wife and co-founder of my company, Eileen, and our Number One mentor and friend, the hugely successful copywriter Russ von Hoelscher.

Then I'll go over a series of methods that you can use to put those answers to use in your day-to-day business life. Think of this report as the equivalent of a website's FAQ page, it answers a series of Frequently Asked Questions that can help you get on the straight and narrow and keep you there as you work your way toward riches. And believe this: it will be work. A lot of it. **Unless you're the heir of a rich and powerful family, no one's going to just give you the money you want.**

Each one of the methods I review here is tried and tested, and while not every single one will necessarily work for you, I'm confident you'll find a few gems here that you can use -- and probably more than a few. **Taken together, they'll help you build an effective framework to prepare you for the process of hacking your way through the business jungle toward the treasure that lies at trail's end.**

So let's get right down to it: What does it take to start a million dollar business? Turn the page and find out!

Part One

Q&A

As an information marketing specialist, I earn most of my money by helping other people make money. In fact, that's our motto at M.O.R.E. Inc.: **"Our Business Has Been Making People Money Since 1988."**

Probably the most common question I'm asked is simply this:

What advice would you give to new clients who want to make millions of dollars?

In a sense, this is a loaded question, and I could spend a hundred pages answering it alone. But what it all boils down to is something very elementary: **Go into business for yourself**. Start a business of your own, whether part-time or full-time. Your chances of getting rich are very slim if you're working for other people, so you must think in terms of making money for yourself if you want to be truly successful.

One reason most people don't start a business is because they have a sense of security in their present job. They might not like their job, they might not like their boss, and they might not like anything else about the situation, but they feel secure. But when we see AT&T and IBM and all these other big companies laying people off, the truth becomes obvious: **there's no security in working for someone else, ever**. The greatest security is to do something for yourself.

Years ago, the ambition bug bit me and I decided to make a lot of money. I told my Dad, "I just want to be a millionaire. I want to get rich." I started sending away for all these get-rich-quick books. He saw me spending all my extra money, and all my extra time thinking about making a lot of money. One day he got very frustrated with me and told me, "Son, you better get all these ideas out of your head. There are only two ways to get rich: you have to either marry it, or you have to inherit it. You're sure not going to inherit it, so get all these stupid ideas about making a lot of money out of your head."

Well, he was wrong, because the third choice is to start a business.

Whatever you decide to sell, make sure it's something that really excites you. That will help keep you excited during the times that are not so exciting, when you're performing some of the drudgery you'll encounter in all business ventures and when things aren't going as well as you had hoped at first. **There'll be ups and downs; business is always a process of couple steps forward and a step back, so you need to be doing something you like, so you'll stay enthused.**

Now, if you want to make millions of dollars, you have to find ideas that are capable of generating that kind of money. **If you can't think of anything on your own that you believe might be profitable, don't give up -- seek out high-profit ideas that others are using right now.** Gain an intimate knowledge of what these other individuals and companies are doing to make their millions of dollars. Learn to compete very strongly with those companies and individuals that are already making millions of dollars. **Don't copy them, but strive to do the same kinds of things they're doing -- only a little differently**. Maybe you can find the weak areas that could be improved upon, or add a new twist no one has taken advantage of in the past. In any case, dedicate yourself to becoming a leader in the field. **One important thing to remember is that in order to move forward, you have to starting bringing in the money first so you can keep going and expand in the directions you need to go**. Sometimes, I think people get too caught up in the methods without worrying about where the money's coming from and that's the fault of most of the business and money-making books that are available out there. They talk too much about how to organize things, mostly because they're written by people who are upper-level company managers. They have no idea anymore (if they ever did) of what it's like to be down there in the trenches, actually doing the things you have to do bring in the bucks. **The truth is, you've got to bring the bucks in first before you can manage the whole thing.**

Russ von Hoelscher has a lot of clients who come to him after they get started. Here's a particularly egregious example: one guy wanted to manufacture some items and import others from Taiwan. He set everything up before he even made a penny. He had about 10,000 square feet of warehouse space in Chicago and he'd put in the finest computers in his offices -- even before he had a clue what, exactly, he was going to do. **He had invested $48,000 by then, with more going down the pipe, because he had this ongoing lease arrangement to deal with**. Well...that's just not the way to do it. As my friend and colleague Alan Bechtold puts it, "It doesn't matter what kind of trouble you get into, and it doesn't matter what kinds of things you come up against, as long as you have the money to deal with them." Well, in order to have that money, you have to earn it first.

Once you've set up the framework of your business in

a way that'll keep you passionate and solvent, consider the implementation side of the equation. I believe that, first of all, you need to get the help of a good copywriter -- a really effective, legitimate copywriter, the very best you can afford, unless you're already a brilliant copywriter in your own right. Second, I think you should put a customer service line together, whether it's open for two or three hours a day or all day long. You need this element so that people can call in and find out you're a real person, you're a real good company, and so they can get help whenever they need it. A customer service line cuts down on complaints. It will also help you build, and maintain, a good customer base, which will be one key to your ultimate success.

Question #2 is this: What's the best way I can get started right now?

That's an easy one -- because the best way to get started is just to start. That sounds simplistic, I know, but it's something you have to do; I think procrastination keeps too many people from being successful. **In the classic words of Nike, the shoe company: Just Do It.** Find something you like to do and think about how you could build it into a successful enterprise. Don't just think about the money, though that's important. **It's most important, at the beginning, to feel comfortable, to feel excited, to be enthusiastic, and to really be passionate about what you're doing.**

Now, it's true that you have to learn before you earn. That means you have to study the good books on marketing and running a business. You need to listen to audiotapes and CDs by business experts. But eventually, and as soon as possible once you have this elementary learning, you've got to take positive action. **You've got to absolutely get up off your duff and do something.** Create something to sell, or get products and services from others that give you a good mark-up. Then you have to get busy marketing them. You have to realize that once you start, the job is really in full-swing. Just go out there and do it.

The second one piece of advice I have is, start small and get your feet wet. You can do that either by being a distributor or starting with your own thing. Start small with something you can do part-time, to check it out, to see if being your own boss is right for you. If you're envisioning a direct response marketing business, once you've decided what you'll sell, start out by running small classified ads, and pyramid the profits that come in. Don't take the money out of your retirement fund or anything like that, just so you can start with a bang; you may end with a whimper. **Start small so you can feel comfortable in the beginning.**

Here's another important point: Quit waiting for that perfect time. What I mean by that is this: A lot of people, millions of people, want to start businesses. You could go out on the street and ask a hundred people, "Have you ever thought about starting your own business?" and out of those one hundred people, probably ninety of them would answer, "You bet I've thought about it." **But the problem is, a lot of people are waiting for that perfect time and it just never happens.** In fact, the perfect time will never come on its own; you've got to make your perfect time.

Question #3 is: Do you have a million dollar plan for starting a business that you can give me?

That's a tough one, but I take it to the basics and then it becomes a little easier. Again, I think you should do what you love to do. You're going to do so much better when you enjoy what you're doing. With a direct response business (which I believe is the best way to go), find something you're excited about and start to invest in it in a small way. **First, try to learn how to make $100**. I've talked about that in other publications; it's one of the basic steps to success in this business. **You learn how to make a small profit, and then you multiply your direct mail, your classified, display, or electronic advertising, or a combination of those things, along with maybe television or radio in the future, as you build up your profits.** You just continue to make money doing what you like, finding a way to make a small profit that you can plow back into the business. This is what I mean by "pyramiding."

Direct response marketing is so exciting because if you make a small profit, and if the market is big enough, there's no reason you can't multiply it by ten, twenty, or one hundred times and build it into a million dollar business. We've done it at M.O.R.E. Inc. **What you have to do is find something people need or want and then fulfill that desire.** Find a way to give them what they want. At the same time, give them what they need, in the form of a good, solid product or service. It doesn't have to be fancy, as long as it's something that people desire, something that fills a want or need.

Don't be a generalist. **Seek out a specific market and study that market closely.** When my wife Eileen and I founded M.O.R.E. Inc., we weren't just striking out blind. We already knew a lot about the market we were in before we got started, so we were able to start with a few hundred dollars and turned it into millions in just a few years. We were buying a lot of different moneymaking plans and programs. We were involved in so many different ways of making money ourselves that we had a very strong knowledge of the people in this market. We knew who was selling the types of products that we wanted to create for others and we knew very well all the problems with those products. We knew what was good, and what excited people, because we were already so close to being our model customers ourselves.

That's critical. When you can understand your potential customers, and model their needs, wants, and desires to the nth degree, you create a bond between you and them. **You understand their hopes, desires, fears, and apprehensions.** Then it becomes so much easier to target your information or products right to that marketplace.

Question 4 is: What do you say to people who are holding back from going into business for themselves because they're afraid?

This is something we see a lot of: People are just afraid to go into business for themselves. Maybe they don't want to admit it, but fear is something we all have to deal with. I've already touched on this briefly, and I'll stick with what I told you then: face your fear and do it anyway. **The reason I say that is because there's nothing in life that's 100% secure.** But I do think there's a lot more security in learning a business, learning your marketplace, and learning to do something you like to do, than to be stuck in any job. So again I would just say: face your fear, but start a business anyhow. **Just Do It.** Learn to take that first baby step. No matter what you try to do, it's all foreign to you in the beginning; but that will certainly change. Read, learn, and study. I've noticed in my lifetime that everything I think is tough becomes easy once I start to do it regularly.

Time's a-wastin', folks. I often tell people, "You're never going to be as young as you are today. You're never going to have as much energy as you have today." **It doesn't matter if you're thirty or forty or fifty, today is the only day you're going to have this much energy, so just go ahead and do it.** That's what you need to do: go ahead and do it. Get out there and do something.

You can always hire accountants to tell you what taxes you need to pay and help you keep your books straight. You can always hire attorneys to avoid legal problems or to help you with any legal problems you might get into. **You can always get outside help for almost everything.** Here's an example. I hadn't seen a good friend of mine, for about ten or fifteen years, when Eileen and I ran into him at a restaurant a few years ago. It turned out he'd started a business that deals with government contracts and he'd made a real success out of it. He'd heard about our success and we'd heard about his. So I asked him, "How in the world did you get into this business?" His business deals with all kinds of complicated government and insurance company contracts. He has a huge staff of people. He said, **"I did it the same way you guys did it. I just got into it and I learned it as I went along."**

I know that sounds like a cliché or a pat answer, but I think that, too often, people see entrepreneurs as being a fearless breed of people. **They see us taking huge risks and they seem to think that entrepreneurs are different from everyone else.** But my friend hit it right on the head. You learn it as you go along and it all gets easier as you do it. It always does.

I used to think I was brilliant because everything I got involved in became easier. But then, as I've met other entrepreneurs, they tell me that's true for them too. So, shucks, I guess I'm not as brilliant as I thought I was! It's just a human thing. Once you do it regularly, any task becomes easier.

One of the biggest hypes out there is when people pretend they know all the answers and you can never learn them. **Sometimes we buy into that and say, "Oh, I could never do that!" But once you start to do it, you say, "Hey! This wasn't half as hard as I thought it would be."** Now, there are times in my past that I wouldn't want to live through again because I've gone through so many business headaches, but I've learned so much from those times that when these problems come along again, I'll know how to deal with them. <u>Not only do you gain the knowledge you need, you gain confidence as you go.</u> Again, I think a lot of people don't realize that all entrepreneurs have to deal with the same kinds of fears, insecurities, and doubts that they do. But they learn to make friends with their fear. They don't let their fear beat them or destroy them. They continue to move forward.

Here's another quick tip: do the tough things first. I've learned this lesson over the years. You know, sometimes we start to bite around the edges of a task or some important things we have to do. We take the easy things first. **But if you do the tough ones first, if you make the phone call that you really don't want to make, or do whatever you just don't want to do, then it's all downhill after that**.

Somebody gave us some good advice early on: we learned that in the direct response marketing business you write the ad first. **Put all your energy, all your initial enthusiasm, everything into all your sales material and then develop from there.** By doing that you commit yourself, for one thing. As soon as the sales material is done, you have to put everything else together. There's a commitment, and that helps get you started.

Question #5: What success stories can I offer of people who have started from scratch and have now built million dollar businesses?

I have many. There's us (Eileen and I), of course. Here's another: Twenty years ago, a guy in Minnesota was working in a government position for the Fish and Game Department, but his hobby was making fishing lures. He finally came up with this lure that had a plastic silicone covering; inside were bright reds, blues, oranges, and yellows. It would twist and turn in the water, and fish just went crazy for it. Russ von Hoelscher knew his son, so he asked for Russ' help at that time to start a company called the Sky Blue Water Company. He ended up making a lot of money with that particular fishing lure, and then dozens and dozens of others that he created. **He turned his hobby into a multi-million dollar business and then sold it to a tackle company years later.** This shows you how your hobby can be where you make your millions.

Then there's the story about another good friend of Russ' that he worked with for years -- George Stern, a marvelous guy. He was a broker in an insurance company. He decided he had to get a list of financial planners 14 or 15 years ago because he wanted to sell some insurance products to these people, or get them to sell for him. **He wanted to rent a list for just the San Diego area, but he had to take the whole state of California, because that's how they sold the list.** He got his list, and could only use ninety percent. He started to make some phone calls to people he knew in Los Angeles, Sacramento, San Francisco, and San Jose. <u>He ended up selling the rest of the list to these other people who could use these names; in the end, he made two or three times the price of the list.</u> Within a couple years, he was on his way to a multimillion dollar list business with doctors, nurses, lawyers, and all other kinds of professions besides financial planners. **In this case, it all started by accident when he figured out a way to sell those extra names rather than throw them away.** It just shows you that you should always be alert to opportunities that surround you because sometimes you never plan for the best opportunity that shows up.

Here's a story about a man we met not long after we got our own business off the ground. **I'll never forget the guy because he looked just like a regular guy who marched along the river with his fishing pole.** I was kind of surprised by that. Anyhow, this guy started out with a number of little businesses; I guess he went bankrupt with a couple of them. **But today he has a multimillion dollar business selling computers and the business opportunities to go with them.** This company brings in millions of dollars a month. This guy works three weeks and then takes three weeks off. We all know we have to work when we run a business, but otherwise, I'd say he lives the "life of Riley." He's really made his mark. The last time I talked to him, he was bringing in $36 million a year. Four million of that was pure profit that was going right into his pocket.

In his case, he got into computers because he was in a related business before that; he started in computer dialers, those machines that call people and do telemarketing with a machine. Then, as government regulatory agencies started cracking down on that type of marketing, he started looking for other computer-related things to do. **Again, it was a natural extension of something that he was already doing.**

In this case, and the George Stern example, we're talking about people who thought bigger than average folks.

That's a good characteristic to have; it's so important to think big. **Another thing we can learn from this, too, is to learn to "catch a wave."** Always look for that hot new trend, because we know that the Ross Perots of this world (and the Bill Gateses) have made not just millions of dollars, but billions of dollars by successfully catching those hot waves. One of the hot waves today is, of course, computers. Another is online marketing.

Also, you need to have something unique. Eileen and I have a friend in Birmingham, Alabama, who started a mail order business just a few years earlier than we started ours. Although Jim has never really been interested in making tens of millions of dollars, he and his wife are bringing in over $100,000 a month in a good month right now. It's just Jim, his wife, and one full-time employee running the whole thing. The employee doesn't actually work for Jim; he works for a temporary help service. **The secret to Jim's success is the fact that he came up with something unique, just like Eileen and I did.** That's one of our guiding principles: find something unique. When Eileen and I started with our $300 ad, we came out with a unique idea. That's what Jim has. I can't mention what he's selling, but he's in the same market we're in. Every month he runs a certain number of ads in all the opportunity magazines and also does some direct mail, and every month he's bringing in between $50,000 and $100,000. This goes to show the power of direct response marketing, especially when you come out with something that's different than anything else out there.

Question #6: If you could give me just a few strategies for making millions of dollars, what would they be?

Well, that's a tough one. I'll go over nine items here, many of which are interrelated, all of which we've used at

M.O.R.E. Inc. from the very beginning. **First of all, study a target market.** You need a market that's big enough so you know there are enough people you can sell to, but not so big that it's hard to reach. Learn everything you can about it. **Second, put together a great information product that's right for the market you've studied, learned about, and know like the back of your hand**. I believe this is a great way for the "little people" to get rich. **Third, Get involved in the mail order/direct response business.** I think it's the greatest business in the world.

Fourth: Give people what they want, not what you want -- or what you think they want. The only way you'll sell is to offer them exactly what they desire. **Fifth, make it a pleasure to do business with your company. And Sixth, be sure to duplicate your efforts with direct mail**. Don't recreate the wheel every time and always multiply your efforts once you've identified something successful.

Number Seven is something I've already said before, but I'll repeat it for emphasis. **You must be in business for yourself.** You can't expect anybody to pay you millions of dollars as an employee. There are very few Lee Iacoccas out there. **Eighth: you have to think big**. Don't sweat the small stuff. And finally, realize that the "why" to make millions of dollars is more important than the "how" to make millions of dollars. You have to have a lot of reasons if you want to go out and make a lot of money. Exactly how you're going to do it can all be figured out slowly as you go along.
I first heard that last item, Number Nine, on a motivational tape -- and I guess like a lot of things that you hear on those tapes or read in motivational books, it sounds clever. I really didn't think about it much at the time, but since then, I've spent a lot of time thinking about it. Everybody wants to know: How do we go about making all our money? Just as Earl Nightingale once said on the "Strangest Secret," a very

popular talk that he once gave, **I tell them: "You have to have strong reasons for wanting something.** Once you have those strong reasons and you set your goals, then you'll find the ideas. They'll naturally come to you."

Here's another thing I'll share with you before I move on. Every morning I try to spend some time by myself. **By that, I mean that I just simply sit down with a tablet and a cup of coffee and let ideas come to me.** It's amazing, in that quiet time when you're really determined to do something and you're determined to be successful, how something inside you will bring those ideas through. Then if you capture them on paper, you can learn a lot. It's tremendous.

You need to know why you want to be rich; just making a lot of money is not enough. **You have to have a reason to make the money.** And you need to know what you want to do with the money. That motivates you and keeps you going when the going gets tough. Once I was talking to my sister about money and she said, "I don't want to make a million dollars. I don't have any use for a million dollars. I just want to be able to pay my bills." And I told her, **"If you only want to pay your bills, that's all you're going to get. Don't worry; if you don't want to make millions, you won't make millions."** That might have sounded self-righteous, but it goes right in line with what we're saying here. Nobody will figure out how to make millions of dollars unless they set out with that goal in mind.

One thing I need to add is: When you talk about getting rich, that's very subjective. **Being rich to one person means something different than what being rich means to another person.** But when you talk about making millions, you're talking more about a set amount. It costs money to make money and to keep making money every day of every year. It will cost money to roll that money back over. So it'll take some time to put a million dollars into your bank account because you're mostly putting it back into your business, hopefully. **You need a purpose for your money.** That purpose can be a beautiful house that you visualize. It could be a trip to Europe. It can be money for college for the kids. It could be to build a business that you'll hand down to your children.

There has to be a "why," a reason for the money. Then there has to be a plan that gets the money and you have to visualize why you want it or what you're going to do with it. **Money doesn't just come to you for no apparent reason.** You have to do something for that money and have a plan for what you'll do with it.

Question #7: How do I find the highest-profit idea that will make me millions of dollars?

This is another tough one because I think the best, highest-profit idea can be different things to different people because, frankly, we all come into the game equipped in various ways by our educations, experiences, and general personality. **If you're involved in direct response marketing, then I think you should start with information products, thinking in a big, big way (even if you start small)**. If you want to get the most profit from your idea don't think, for example, about putting together a book. A book has a perceived value. It might be $10; it might be $20; it might even be $40. But even so, there's a limit to how much money you can make with a book. We've written and sold dozens and dozens of books, one at a time. **Although we profited from it, we became far more prosperous when we**

realized that it's much better to put together a home study course or a multi-product offer. By that, I mean you might have a book, a set of cassette tapes or CDs, maybe videos, reports, or maybe even a newsletter in the package. In other words, you enhance your offer by making it very comprehensive.

Then, instead of $20, $40, or $50, you're offering so much value to the potential customer that you can charge $200, $300, $400, or more. **You'll enrich yourself, but you'll also enrich the customer because you cover all aspects of the topic and you give them the information they absolutely need to have.** That seems to be a key to getting rich: empowering other people by adding value to their lives. To do so with a comprehensive program, as opposed to just a booklet or a book in the field of information selling, is the way to enrich the other person while you enrich yourself.

In addition, for the highest profit, I think you need to have the lowest initial cost. This includes paper and ink, audio CDs, and CD-ROMs, all of which are very low-cost in and of themselves. **It's the information you put on them, whatever that might be, that has the real value**. Even if you're not selling informational products, you have to sell low cost, high-profit items to make real money. That is to say, they cost you very little; but their value to the prospect or customer is perceived by them to be very high.

Question #8 in our FAQ: What's the single most important lesson you've learned from making millions of dollars?

You know, if all these questions were easy, this report

would be about three pages long. Here's another toughie! So many things contribute to a person's success. **When I was thinking about this recently, a popular marketing cliché came to mind: "Find a need and fill it."** Like most clichés, there's some truth to that. It's very important to find a good market and then to develop products for that market. Once you know that there's a market with a sufficient number of people who can use certain types of products, whether they're informational products or "hard" products, you need to start planning ways to effectively target that market. Once you know the right type of merchandise or information to sell to that market, then you just keep developing products for those customers. **Eventually, if you have enough of a customer base and you develop enough different products and services for that customer base, then you can get rich.**

The single most important thing I've learned is this: I set out some years ago with a goal of making a lot of money, but I just didn't know how. **When I was sitting around wishing that we could make millions of dollars, I never realized that all that money I so desperately wanted at the time and didn't know how to get was out there right then**. Well, they're still out there right now waiting for clever marketers to claim them. The key to getting those millions of dollars is to get the right offer to the right market through the right medium at the right time.

Just keep this in mind, always: the most important people in the world are your customers. You can probably make ten times more money re-selling to your existing customers than you can by constantly trying to sell to new people. **Sure, you want to bring new people in with your lead-generation, but by working your customer file you can maximize your profits.** These people know you, know the kinds of products you sell, and know you delivery good products with excellent customer service (both of which are absolutely necessary if you want to succeed). With that in mind, you should also plan for rainy days. In our business, we seem to have severe ups and severe downs. **You always need to plan and understand that you might be running high today, but you're likely to hit the bottom again.** Also, hire as many good people as you can whenever you need them, people like attorneys, accountants, CPAs -- specialists who really know their jobs.

Question #9: What's the fastest way you know of to make the most money?

I still think the fastest way is the old-fashioned way, even with all this newfangled technology that lets us pursue high-tech options like electronic and television marketing. **You find or create a hot product or service that you can market by direct mail.** You can get mailing lists that target your market, you can get your product out in the mail quickly, and you can get your response quickly. When you place ads in magazines, it can take two, three, sometimes even four months for that ad to appear. The quickest, fastest, and often the best way is the good old-fashioned post office. **Direct mail is also a low-risk method if you work it right, which is what makes it so beautiful.** You can make a small test; mail toa couple of thousand people first. If you're successful, and if the market is big enough, you can be mailing 50,000 to 100,000 in no time at all. You can pyramid your profits: take the profits from one mailing and perhaps double the size of the second mailing and the third and fourth. I'm a big, big advocate of using direct mail to test and to roll out for profits.

And let me re-emphasize something I've already covered a couple of times: the fastest and easiest way

to make money is to not work for somebody else. It's not to have a nine-to-five job. It's to start something on your own and just go for it. **Hopefully, you'll use direct mail in whatever you do because direct mail is like having 100, 1,000, or 10,000 people just like you out there knocking on people's doors.** It's an amplified method of selling -- what the military calls a "force multiplier" -- that lets you effectively be in business for yourself. If you don't go into business for yourself, none of these principles will apply as well, unless of course you use them for your boss's benefit. Maybe he'll promote you and give you raises. That would be nice, but to make maximum money in the minimum time, you just have to have a business of your own; you have to control your destiny.

Like I shared earlier, it's not nearly as difficult to work for yourself as people think, especially once you get past the first hurdle -- <u>that hurdle being just getting started and learning some of these initial things.</u> We have people come to us all the time and say, "Man, if I just knew how easy it was, I would have done it a long time ago." My wife, Eileen, talked to one of our customers a while back, someone who had started a mail order business and experienced some problems early on. He had started his business when he was nineteen or twenty and he's in his sixties now. He said the first time he started it, he got a postal notice: cease and desist. **He got in a little trouble with the government, which happens to most people every once in a while.** Well, I wouldn't call it trouble; it was just a form letter. He told me that if he had known then what he knows today, he would still be doing that same thing because he knew he wasn't doing anything wrong. He wouldn't have let something small stop him.

That brings me right to Question #10 because it does involve legal situations and it's something a lot of people are curious about.

The question is this: What are your best ideas for avoiding all legal problems?

I think it gets down to the basics. **First of all, make sure your offers are truthful.** If you're telling people you can make $5,000 a day with this opportunity, you better have been making $5,000 a day or have written testimonials on file from people who are making $5,000 a day using your plan or a similar one. In other words, you have to tell the truth and you have to back it up. **Second, no matter how good the products you're selling are, some people will send them back for refunds.** Some people will copy them and then send them back. It's not always your fault; often, the customer's just looking to get something for nothing. Now, you don't get a lot of refunds if you have good products, but you will get some no matter what. **When the request comes in, you have to make the refund.** The only way that you can get by without making a refund is if you put a disclaimer in your ad or sales letter saying something like this: We do not give refunds. Let me tell you something, friends; if you put that in there, you don't have to make refunds, but you also won't get many orders.

Another thing: know if you're selling something sensitive. Some people get involved in health information, which is a very lucrative field. I've seen problems with people I know who are selling things like cures for cancer or arthritis. You have to be very careful. The AMA (American Medical Association) is a very powerful organization in America. Right or wrong, they will not stand for anyone who says you can cure this disease or that one. On the other hand, you can say this has helped people; there are ways to word your message, but you can't talk about outright cures.

But keep this in mind: it can be very hard, at times, to stay within the legal lines because those lines can move -- and where they lie, sometimes, is entirely subjective. **You can try and try to stay legal, but if the government reinterprets what's considered legal and isn't you can get into trouble fast -- especially in regards to the advertising that you put out to the public.** If you can't stand behind that advertising and show that it's 100% truthful, then you're going to be in trouble. I once read in a law book that the FTC (which monitors all advertising) once pulled all Kraft cheese TV commercials because they claimed Kraft was lying in their advertisements. Sometimes, they'll even go after small things that they can nit-pick on.

Handle all government agencies promptly -- <u>any inquiries</u>. Do not hide under the table. Do not throw them in the trash. Just handle them in as straightforward a manner as you can. You may not even be in trouble; sometimes when people are investigating you, they just want to know what you're doing. They just have to have something on you in their file. **If they have consumers calling them asking about your company, they have to know what your company does**. When you're in this business to make a lot of money and you're sending out millions of pieces of mail and you're running ads everywhere and the profits are great, you're also going to draw some attention to yourself. So get local training to give you some advice on how to handle routine inquiries. **However, you also need to know what kind of attorneys to get for certain kinds of problems.** A local attorney can't go to bat for you with postal authorities, for example, they don't have the knowledge. You may have to reach far afield for a specialist, though you can usually find one in a big city.

Nobody wants legal problems, but when you're

going for the big bucks, you have to accept the fact that you'll find yourself in a certain number of legal situations. A few years back, Eileen and I were at the Kansas State Fair in Hutchinson, Kansas. The Consumer Protection Bureau for the Attorney General's office had a booth set up and I got to spend about 10 minutes talking to their representative while Eileen was in the booth next door, buying shoes. This guy has a pretty powerful position. He, of course, knew of our company because we're a mail order company in a small state. **Basically, these government regulatory agents, as he expressed to me, aren't in business to shut anybody down; they're pro-business**. They're just trying to do their jobs. As long as you pay your refunds and you simply do what you're supposed to do, there will be no serious repercussions. If you make claims on earnings, as we often do, you have to back them up -- because eventually someone's going to say, "You said you made $5 million last year. Where's the proof of that claim?" <u>As long as you have the proof, there's no problem.</u>

Here's another thing to be wary of: anyone in the direct response mail order business gets solicited for chain letters. You put your name in the #5 slot, then you move to #4 if you send $5 here, $5 there, $3 here, and $3 there. **Take it from someone who knows better: don't do it. Don't get involved. I've never heard of anyone making money with this.** In fact, 99% of these chain letters are outright illegal. There's no such person as Edward Green. Who's that, you might ask? Why, Edward Green is that mythical person who's made a pile of money from his chain letter and who's out playing on the beach at Maui. When I first thought about getting involved in mail order twenty-five or thirty years ago, I received an Edward Green letter. Now it's almost thirty years later and the last one I received was last week. It's the same old story, with the same old name: and it's just a bunch of bologna.

Question #11 is this: How can somebody turn their own really great idea into a million dollar business?

A great idea can lead to great riches; there's no question about it. **Every business success starts with a great idea.** I'm being a bit redundant, I know, but let me emphasize again that you have to find the market first. Then you have to find out what other people are doing to serve that market. Then you have to think about what you could do to offer products and services that are similar, but even better than your competitors'. **Find a unique selling position, a USP, that gives you an advantage over the competition, because you do something better than anyone else does.**

So find that target market, but not a huge market that you can't define. **If the market is everybody, then the market is really nobody.** Your market may be photographers, hunters, fishermen, or opportunity seekers, but it has to be someone you can zero in on. **Sometimes people fall in love with their ideas to the extent that they think almost everybody is going to be a potential customer for their product or service**. When that happens, it's a prescription for disaster because we need target markets. We're not General Motors or General Mills. We're not selling cars and cereals to everyone across the nation. We want a niche market big enough that so we can make plenty of profits, but we don't want markets that are everybody. Why? Because they're too hard to reach.
Once you've found that market, learn to be process-oriented. **The best ideas that we've had so far, the ones that have made us all our money, have come as a result of a process.** Ideas are like little babies. They need to be treated lightly and you need to play with them and take good care of

them. Sometimes the best ideas are those that come as the result of working through other ideas and learning from them. I often tell people that only about one out of ten of our ideas are any good. But if we can make millions of dollars from that one out of ten, then all we need is just a few of those ideas every few years and we're fine. Just realize that product development is a process. That idea has to grow. It has to build and expand. <u>The best ideas come as a result of serving your customers because the more you service your customers, the more you find out what their needs are -- and the more you're able to come up with those really powerful ideas that can make you a lot of money.</u>

Question #12: What are the top reasons you believe it's possible for the average person to get rich?

You really just need a big dream, a big idea, and a burning desire to succeed. I've seen so many people do it that I know it's true. There was a success story in the San Diego paper about ten years ago about a gentleman who came over from Vietnam, flat broke, as one of the boat people back in the mid-1970s. He worked for six years as a dish washer at a restaurant, several restaurants. Well, the story said he'd bought something like $22,000,000 worth of ocean-front commercial property in San Diego. In 1974, he had zero capital; today he's a multimillionaire.

In direct response marketing, I could name hundreds of people I've known and have had dealings with who've gone from rags to riches. **So there's no question that if you believe you can do it, if you get excited about it, you can do it.** Part of that's because we have one of the world's best countries to live in. We have all these people coming into this country who don't even know how to speak our language, but they succeed and add to our culture tremendously because they believe they can do it. They're here in America, the land of opportunity. You can do it. Maybe you were born here in America and you don't dare believe you can. **But think of it: if foreigners who come across the ocean to our country can make millions of dollars, you can do it, too**. And despite common belief, it's not necessarily because they're getting special favors.

A belief that you can do it should always fuel your business efforts. Without that, a book like this one is worthless -- because you absolutely have to believe it's possible. So the more people who do it, the more average, regular people go out there and make millions, the more it helps other people. It helps to pave that path to riches.

Part Two

Putting the Answers to Work

In this section, I'll discuss some basic business plans that you can use starting out with just $1,000, $500 -- even just $100! Put them to proper use and you can eventually have your own million dollar business. Here's where I'll really go into detail on the answers I supplied in the last section.

The Inadequacies of Business Books

A few years ago, Eileen and I took the day off and went to Wichita, which is the biggest city in this area, and we shopped around. We went to a huge bookstore in Wichita that we've been to before. They have probably four or five aisles of business books alone. Eileen and I have a whole library full of these books, but we're always looking for something new. Well, after about an hour of looking through these books and trying to find something different and good, I became really depressed -- because all these books are the same. **It really upsets me to think that many of the people out there looking for a way to make more money go first to the library or the bookstore**. One of the things I thought about before I started working on this publication was the fact that most of these books are either written by CEOs of big corporations or they're written by managers: people who manage other people's businesses. They're complicated and full of all kinds of junk.

In this publication -- and the rest of the publications and programs we produce here -- we show you how we've actually done it. We started dirt poor and we've built a million dollar business. I think that's so much different from a lot of the stuff that's out there. Now, it's all right to read books on management, even though most of the information they cover is written for people who are working in big corporations. **It really doesn't apply to the entrepreneur who's making a boot-strap start with a very limited amount of money.** Most of the businesses you read about in these books would require $100,000 just to set up the business, much less get it started.

All these books have some good things in them, but what bothers me is that they tend to complicate what it takes to make money, compared to what we've found out for ourselves. **It's irritating to see so many people being misled and I think it scares a lot of people away from getting into business for themselves, if only because these books emphasize these long lists of what you "have" to do before you get into business.** The truth is, the best way to get into business is to do some research and then just to start. Just do it. Things don't have to be perfect; in fact, things never are.

Getting Started: Just Do It

When people ask, "How much money does it take to get started in business?" I tell them, **"A lot less than you think, especially if you start part-time."** Some people ask, "Can you start with $100?" I've told people for years that's how Russ von Hoelscher started: part-time with $100, and look at him now. Now admittedly, that was over thirty years ago, so $100 then would be comparable to $500 or more today. That being the case, to really start a business part-time, I think you have to have $500 or $1,000, even if it's a direct response business. Let's face it: postage stamps cost 42 cents. Back thirty-plus years ago, they were something like 5 or 6 cents. **That's why I recommend you have $500 or $1,000 or more to start a business. If you've got that kind of wherewithal, you can easily start part-time, at your kitchen table, like so many of us did**. Eileen and I started that way and so did Russ. Just get involved in something good. Of course, in our direct response business, we're always talking about selling information because we love that.

Your informational products don't have to be beautiful works of art. They may be booklets you've copied at the local quick printer and stapled together yourself. But if there's good information there, people will be happy to receive your items and they'll keep them. So you can easily start your business part-time for $1,000 or less, although having a little more certainly is necessary if you're going to do big mailings or place larger ads.

Where do you get that seed money? **Well, most people don't realize that they probably have several thousand dollars worth of things they could potentially sell to raise money.** We talk to people all the time on the telephone who tell us they're broke. Then we get to counseling with these people, and find that they do have a second car they don't drive very often that they could sell. Or they have some old stereo equipment back from when that was their hobby. **If the desire is there, most people can raise the kind of money they need to start out with by doing lots of buying and selling and wheeling and dealing.** Now, if you don't have the desire to make money for yourself, enough desire to dig up that funding, forget it -- because the #1 ingredient in entrepreneurial success, in my opinion, is the desire to succeed. If you have that desire, you'll find the money because you'll sell that second car.

You'll sell that old photography equipment. You'll sell the stereo. You'll get rid of all sorts of stuff that you're probably are not using.

Here's another thing I always tell people: getting involved in a low-cost distributorship is a great way to get your feet wet. A distributorship doesn't require nearly as much money to get started as most other opportunities. A lot of services are offered, like drop-ship, where you get the order first and you get paid for it first. Then you ship the order to the company and they drop-ship for you. So you don't have an inventory to buy, either, and you're fine as long as you're dealing with a good company that sells good stuff and gives you a nice profit margin. **You don't want to fool around with a deal where you're selling something for $10, you keep $5, and you have to run all kinds of ads.** You can lose money that way. Working with a distributorship can be great when you get a good mark-up, but always remember to put 80% of your profits back into advertising, so you have money to grow on.

I don't know who started the big misconception that the #1 reason businesses fail has to do with under-capitalization, but we see this all the time. These so-called experts claim that most people just don't have enough money before they get started. **We've read lots of business books that tell you that you need six months of money to live on before you even start a business**. I don't really believe that; in fact, a lot of the time, the problem is the exact opposite. A successful entrepreneur named Paul Hawkin wrote one of the best books on business that I've ever read, Growing Your Own Business, and he claims that the #1 reason businesses fail is that they have too much money. He explains that by simply saying that when you start with hardly anything, then you learn everything from the ground up. You don't have money to throw at your problems;

you have to solve them yourself, with whatever funds and creativity you can apply to the problem. In the process, you learn things about the business that nobody can possibly learn if they have a whole bunch of money to abdicate the work to other people and let them try to solve it.

Whenever people like that do anything, they want to do it "first class." We see so many people who feel they need far more money than they really do need. **Instead of using money you don't have, substitute creative efforts and ideas.** Too much money will get you in trouble every time.

I'm reminded of a story about a guy in Milwaukee who had a restaurant business for many years. He made $100,000 or more a year. It was a successful restaurant: he had about ten employees, including some of his own family. **He finally got sick and tired of the restaurant business, so he went to a few entrepreneurial seminars and decided he wanted to get into mail order.** He sold his restaurant for about $400,000, and then moved to Chicago to help give his daughter a job (she'd just gotten a divorce). He planned to start publishing reports and selling them through mail order.

Well, by the time he got to our friend Russ, saying, "Help! Help!" he'd set up beautiful offices a block of two from the Tribune in Chicago. He'd installed some expensive equipment, including the best computers. He'd hired a manager and a couple other people, plus his daughter. He'd literally put about $30,000-$40,000 into the business -- and when he came to Russ, he admitted, "You know, I don't know exactly what I want to sell. I was going to sell information that teaches people how to get into the restaurant business and how to promote their restaurants, but I don't know if I want to do that now." **Well, it was kind of late to decide that!**

Then there was a guy who came to one of our seminars. He'd already put $200,000 into his office. He'd hired the managers and secretaries, etc., and he still didn't know anything about what he wanted to do. It's sad. **Again, I think some of this indecision stems from those books out there that seriously mislead people into thinking you have to start out with a huge wad of money in order to be successful.** But you know what? When you start with hardly anything, you have to substitute for the money by always figuring out a creative way to do things. **You develop an intimate knowledge of your customers and what they want because there's nobody else to answer the telephone but you**. You develop an intimate knowledge of the day-to-day activities because, again, in the beginning there's nobody else to do the job that you have to do. You learn how to "wear all of the hats."

Then, as you expand and hire, you can train people to do the job right -- and by right, I mean doing it efficiently. Part of the secret to making a profit is to do everything as efficiently as possible. The power is in doing it. Although it's good to plan, and it's good to read, and it's good to know some of the management techniques, the power does not come from thinking about it. **The power comes when you've made a commitment and you say, "I'm going to do it." Then you do it, and you find out you're a lot smarter than you thought you were.** You may think you don't know enough; well, doing it makes you smarter because you're certainly learning. And it's a great way to gain knowledge -- in fact, <u>it's the best way to learn</u>.

We tell people that there's lots of power in getting started. We tell them that they'll be able to figure things out as they go. Sometimes people think that that's just a cliché; it's easy to come up with a silly pat answer for everything and sometimes people think that that's our pat answer. But here's the truth: there have been so many times that Eileen and I didn't know how to do what we started out to do. For instance, when we built this multi-level marketing company, we'd never done that before. We'd been running a mail order company, but we'd never run a multi-level marketing company. There were new problems to deal with. Our computers had to be set up entirely differently. **Everything was new to us, but we learned as we went along.** It's the same with every type of business we've ever done, every kind of new product that we've put together, every new distributorship we've been involved in.

Let's look at M.O.R.E. Inc. When we started that company, we had no computers; we just used typewriters and filing cabinets. Then we got into the computer world, a friend offered to help us with it. We had to ditch our initial computer software and program after six months because it wasn't working, so we went on to another program. **The thing is, you just grow with it. It's a constant upgrading effort. You bloom where you're planted; you start with what you have.** You try to do the best you can with it and you grow and expand, using your profits to build on.

Creating -- or Finding -- Unique Business Opportunities

Speaking of profits, let's talk about some really unique business ideas that people can get involved in. **How does a person start from scratch and build a super-successful business?** I've known lots of people who have needed to do just that, and the same is true of just about any successful entrepreneur. For example: there's a guy named Ted who lived in San Diego thirty or thirty-five years ago and he loved the pristine beaches and the way California was back then. But he saw things he didn't like, including all the people and the traffic and the rising tides. So, finally, he decided he would bail out and move to the Pacific Northwest. He'd taken some vacations there; he loved Washington, Oregon, and Idaho, the beautiful greenery, the clean air. He loved everything about it. He wanted to go to a very small town there and he wondered how he could do it.

Finally, after talking to friends and associates, he realized that a lot of other people were thinking the same thing. He decided to write his own homemade self-published book on living in the Pacific Northwest. Then he used the answering machine, and put little ads in newspapers: the Los Angeles Times, the San Diego Union, the Orange County Register. He offered a free report on moving to the Northwest and living up there and he got a tremendous response. He sent out the report, which told about his book, which sold for something like $19.95. He actually started to make a profit. Better yet, he got all kinds of free publicity, including big huge write-ups in the Los Angeles Times. **He told Russ von Hoelscher that he sold about five hundred books from this one 2/3-page write-up.** He also got a big write-up in the San Diego Union and the San Jose Mercury and the papers in San Francisco and all over the state. Business was just booming.

Russ suggested that he start a newsletter, as a back-up, and he did that. The newsletter soon became profitable. He continued to advertise, especially in California, catching a real core of people who wanted to bail out. They didn't think California was pristine or the "promised land" that it was years ago. Business just boomed for him. He started with his homemade booklet, then the newsletter. With his ads and free publicity, his business just took off, with thousands of people buying the book and thousands of people subscribing to the newsletter. He did this all on a "shoestring" budget. Now every issue of his newsletter talks about a specific area in Washington, Oregon, or Idaho. He picks out a specific area and tells everything about it -- the pros and cons, the schools, the recreation, everything. That gets people excited. A small percentage of his readers, then, decided they wanted to move there. **Next, he deals with real estate agents in those areas that pay him sizeable commissions -- $500, $1,000, or $1,500 -- when they sell property to someone who comes in on a lead from him.** All this started with just about $1,000 and a lot of desire. Now he has a tremendous business that runs on a little bit of advertising, a little bit of word-of-mouth, a lot of free publicity, and just continues to multiply.

This whole concept reminds me of a house that Eileen and I bought in the Ozarks when we first started making a lot of money. We bought this house in a kind of a resort area where people keep houses that they can go to on the weekends. **We thought about doing something very similar to what he was doing: showing people how they could retire to this area and then working out deals with local real estate people, basically brokering real estate.** We thought it would be a great retirement business for us. This same idea could be used in the Southwest or in the south. In fact, there's another entrepreneur up in Redland, California, who started a newsletter called Rural California Living. He said, "Maybe you don't like how big Los Angeles and San Diego and San Francisco have become, but there are hundreds of small, beautiful communities in California." I think this is really a trend and it could be very profitable.

We thought about doing something like this in Mexico, too, because Mexico has always fascinated us. **We see a lot of people selling books about how to move to Mexico. We see the ads running over and over again, <u>so we know it's a popular topic</u>.** That's one of the ways you find out if an idea is good or not. So we've thought about putting together a newsletter that would allow us to travel Mexico and do a lot of writing. We could meet retired people and do little articles on them. We could actually build a subscription base for this thing and maybe develop some other products for it. This whole concept is exciting because a person can literally travel all over America -- or even the whole world-- with this idea. You can use the world as your playground and tell people the best or cheapest places to live.

That's one way to come up with fabulous business ideas: by keeping an ear to the ground and listening to the news. When we first started putting together our How To Make Money on the Information Super-Highway program, we did it because the Internet was in the news all the time and we were very curious about the whole subject. We wanted to know everything about this Information Super-Highway because, every time we turned on the TV, there was a story about the Internet. We wanted to find out how to make money on it; and once we did, we ended up sharing that information with lots of other people. But we also uncovered the problems that people were having. **You know, you can "gain from the pain.**" By that, I mean something like this: when you see the crime rate rising, when you see the inner cities deteriorating, you know a lot of people are saying, "There has to be a better way. I want to get out of this trap." Helping people find a place in rural America is a natural outgrowth of that.

Recently, Eileen and I were brainstorming some new business ideas of our own and we found that they all centered around that very same kind of thing: <u>looking for people who have some type of specific problem and then figuring out a way to solve their problem</u>. One of the ideas Eileen came up with was this: if you go to a state fair or flea market, you'll see hundreds of people who have hobbies where they make craft items. Well, these people have no real centralized way to advertise. **One of Eileen's**

ideas was to connect those people by putting a catalog together where they could actively advertise their products for sale. That's a great idea, by the way: find people who don't know how to capitalize on the talents they have and give them a way to share themselves and their products with other people.

One of the richest people I've ever met was the man I talked about in the previous section, the fellow in Indiana who's making $36 million a year. **He was telling us about one of his ideas and it involves a very simple concept: just find somebody who has a unique idea they're making money with and turn that into a distributorship opportunity.** This guy found a man that had a unique little local business and he was bringing in tremendous profits. Our friend in Indiana was simply going to put together a book and some video tapes so he filmed this guy and tapped into his man's knowledge and skills and everything that this man had learned, then sold that as a business opportunity to all these other people who were looking for an unusual way to make money. **That's one way to use other people's talents to make money -- but remember, you've always got to cut them in on a nice piece of the action.**

Russ once told us the story of a client of his in the Los Angeles area who was involved in real estate for a long time. He did a large number of seminars and also got into infomercials. **Well, he was in his office one day when an Oriental gentleman came in with a whole new approach to copying documents.** He could scan any sort of document onto CD ROMS and diskettes. It was a simple matter to take a whole file cabinet, or ten file cabinets, and put it all on one or two diskettes. Then you could put an index in the front. So a person just plugs into #27 and the lawyer has his clients, or the doctor has his files, or the manufacturer has the customer's file, or whatever the document is.

The gentleman who brought this in cut the real estate man -- Russ' client -- in for a piece of the action. The client told Russ, "Now we're training other people to do this with our software and equipment. We're advertising. We're doing well -- and we're making about one sale a day." Russ said to him, "Well, it does sounds like you're doing well. But just one sale a day -- does that cut it?" The client replied, **"Well, a sale includes books, tapes, all this other good stuff, and the software. It also includes four to five days of training. <u>So one sale a day is $29,900 a day.</u>"**

As you can see, you can use other people's talents to make piles of money. I hear this a lot from importers and exporters. They say if you place ads in the Los Angeles Times or the San Diego Union or a Dallas or Wichita paper -- wherever you are, it doesn't matter -- and say that you're looking for ideas and products, things to sell to other countries, you'll find all sorts of people who have great products and inventions. Of course, you could also be looking for things to sell in this country. **The point is, they may not know beans about marketing -- but you do and you can capitalize on their talent.**

That's another thing you can do: find local businesses that didn't know how to market their business, then step in and help them bring in more business. **There's so much potential in helping people solve their problems; this seems to be another big area where a lot of small business people need all kinds of help**. Businesses sometimes need more help than individuals do and they generally have more money to spend.

The point is this: there are million dollar ideas everywhere. Just keep your eyes open at all times, wherever you go. Good ideas are everywhere. **A lot of people who want to get into business lack ideas and that alone keeps them from the marketplace**. But ideas are everywhere! There are all kinds of places to look for them. Just use the very simple tools that I'll talk about here and you'll have more ideas than you can handle. Then it's just a matter of homing in and choosing the idea you feel will best work for you.

Freedom -- and Power

That approach offers you a lot of freedom in your business life and freedom -- of every sort -- in the most important thing about being in business for yourself. **Being your own boss provides a certain level of self-determination in so many ways that just aren't available for people who have regular jobs.** Sure, most people start businesses just because of the money alone. They're looking for a way to get rich or to have the nice house and the nice cars that equal success to them. Making money and having control of your finances is great, but if you start a successful business, you're also free – free to the extent that you might work just as hard as or (let's be honest) harder than the person who works for someone else for a living. **But you're doing it for yourself so you can explore all kinds of avenues, take time off when you want to, and you can work when you want to.** I've been in this direct response business over twenty years now. I can choose to take a day off any time, but often I'll work until midnight -- so you can make your hours flexible. Another beautiful thing about freedom is this: as this century gets into gear, a lot of things are happening in our world, and even in our great country, that are disturbing. There are a lot of problems in the cities. A lot of people are distrustful of the government and some of the things it's been doing. But having your own business allows you to live where you want to live, especially when you're in this wonderful direct response business. You can be in a big city or in a small town -- wherever you want to go. You can take control over your life. You don't have to answer to the system.

A lot of entrepreneurs now are doing business out of their homes. Imagine never having to leave for work, never physically going out and getting into the car and driving ten or twenty miles to go to some office or factory. Instead, you have breakfast, you take care of whatever family duties arise, then you go to a separate part of the house – I think that's important – and you're doing business for yourself. Now, many of us do have offices and some employees, but there are many successful entrepreneurs who are doing all their work in the home. They might bring one person in to help them.

Talking about freedom reminds me of something that happened a few years back. Boeing, one of the biggest airplane manufacturing plants in Wichita, decided to go on strike. **Those people were out of a job for the next month or so, during that time they spent all their savings and ended up in a big financial mess.** They had no control over their lives; even the employees who didn't vote to strike couldn't work because hundreds of other people did. Contrast this to something Eileen heard from her mother, who lived in Tucson, Arizona, at about the same time. Apparently Microsoft (the big computer software company) decided to come to Tucson and they had 200 job openings to fill so they rented a huge hotel conference center so people who wanted to work for Microsoft could come and apply. Eight thousand people showed up – for 200 jobs! I think that illustrates very well the lack of freedom that comes from trying to get a good job. **Can you imagine that – 8,000 people trying to get 200 jobs?** The same thing is common in states like California. Russ von Hoelscher tells me that

5,000-6,000 people applied for 100 jobs at few years back at a San Diego biochemistry company. Even if you manage to secure one of these scarce, high-paying jobs, you might work for the company ten or twenty years and you might think you're secure -- but you're really not. **Many of these companies don't care a bit about the little guys.**
Let's look at both sides of the coin. Some of these big companies have actually become far more profitable since they scaled down. Part of the scaling down occurred because of the computer and the high technology revolutions, so you can't blame all the companies out there for the downsizing. They couldn't justify keeping on people they didn't need. Let's face it: they want to make a profit, too. And there's something exciting that comes with the high-tech revolution. Think about computer and distribution technology like Federal Express, fax machines, computer modems, and world-wide computer networks. **This technology is part of what's causing big companies to downsize and lay off hundreds of thousands of workers.** But it's that same technology that gives the small entrepreneur, the regular average Joe like you and me, a chance to compete nationwide -- or even worldwide.

Think of it this way: the average desktop computer is 10 or 20 times more powerful than the computers used in World War II -- computers that were 500 times larger. **It's astonishing to realize that the average person now has 100 times more power in that little computer at home than the entire Pentagon had during the Second World War**. Think of all the things you can do with that kind of raw power!

Due to the freedom that our technology offers now, you've literally got abundant money-making opportunity right at your fingertips -- if you're willing to reach out, grab it, and work hard to keep it. Earlier I mentioned working until midnight some nights, which is something that scares some people away from working for themselves. **They think that to have a million dollar business, you've got to work 24 hours a day. That's not really the case, but I do have to say that you're going to have to pay your dues -- and if that's the case, you'd better do it by finding something you enjoy.** I firmly believe that's one of the prerequisites for having a million dollar business. If you're doing something you enjoy, all of a sudden that work's not work anymore. It becomes a challenge, a passion -- or even a hobby. Plus, when you're working at something you enjoy for yourself and your family, you have an enormous feeling of accomplishment. The flame is burning; you have passion; you feel good about yourself. Your self-confidence and self-worth go up. **Most people who work for other companies just put in the time their time, searching for retirement.** But when you do it for yourself -- if you really believe in what you're doing -- then it's a labor of love.

People say to Eileen and me, "I don't understand how you can work together." They tell us, "I could never work with my spouse. We'd be divorced within the first 30 days." **Well, we believe it's a good thing when husbands and wives work together.** We believe that because that's what we've been doing since 1988, when we got married. It's worked well for us, but admittedly it didn't come easily. The first few years were struggles and things were hard. **The secret that Eileen and I have found is that each spouse in the partnership needs to have a different responsibility.** For years, until she was forced to retire for health reasons, Eileen was our CEO, handling all the management and running the day-to-day business operations. I did the advertising and the marketing. Since we had different functions, we didn't get in each other's way like we did when we first started out.

Going back to the subject of freedom, I honestly think having a good marriage can provide a certain level of freedom or security. **My own personal belief is that a business is more than just making money and doing accounting and paperwork and shipping stuff out the doors.** A business is more like a lifestyle. When Eileen and I talk about what a business really is, we compare it to farming because there are so many farmers in our area. Farming is a way of life for these people. It's an around-the-clock thing for most of them. Every morning, at 3:00 in the morning, the dairy farmers are out milking cows. **It's a lifestyle: that's what a business really is to us, something we share, something we do together.**

And keep in mind the fact that with some kinds of businesses, especially the direct response types, you can live anywhere you want to. You can live in a little town in Wyoming; you can live in Chicago; you can go live on the beach. **You can do business literally any place in the world, as long as you have access to the Internet and a good mail service.** Even better, you're not answering to very many other people when you do it. Now, none of us are totally free; I realize that. We're all dependent to some degree on government and the economy. **But if you have a successful direct response business, you'll never have to worry about what's happening in your immediate area**. When things are down over in San Diego, and people are getting laid off, and the aircraft industry is foundering -- well, Russ von Hoelscher isn't worried, because that's only 1% of his business. He's doing business all over the country and all over the world, so this gives him a position of strength.

When you own your own business, you get to be your own kind of person. But when you work at a job, you're at the mercy of your employer and other employees; your life isn't really your own. **When you work at a job and you need**

extra money, you often end up taking a part-time job after your real job, but when you have your own business, all you need to do is get more sales. That's what we call the "X factor." In the first section of this publication I talked about some of the different ideas for making money. The truth is: those are a dime a dozen, as far as I'm concerned. There are so many ways to make money it's not even funny. Once you start looking around and become aware of that fact, you can actually become overwhelmed at times. I like to say, "There are just too many ideas and not enough time."

If nothing else, I hope that's the one thing you've learned after reading this book. **There are opportunities everywhere. You need to realize that if you have a desire, these available opportunities can fulfill that desire.** Look for those opportunities; even use other people's ideas and talents to make money. When you get into this habit of free thinking, you'll be amazed at how ideas will come to you faster than you can even assimilate them. In fact, they come to you so fast that you'll have to pick and choose because there's not enough time to do them all.

Again, the best ideas come as a result of the process of just getting started and working with your customers. I'd like to make a very important point about capitalism here because it's getting a bad rap these days. **There's a real movement against wealthy people who have built successful businesses and now live in nice, fancy homes**. It's envy, really. I think some politicians like to agitate the people who aren't prosperous and I think it's a terribly destructive thing. We ought to look up the successful people and say, "We don't hate you. We want to join you."

To make the most money, you have to serve the most

people. **That's the thing about capitalism that I love: you get rich by enriching the lives of others, by trying to provide products and services that people really need, things that are really going to make a difference in their lives.** That's how you get rich -- not by ripping people off or taking advantage of people or manipulating people; it's trying to figure out how you can serve them. Some of the biggest billion-dollar companies in this country started humbly. **My grandfather knew a man who started a company in the basement of his home in Minnesota, back in the 1920s. Today it's a multibillion-dollar company, one of the ten biggest companies in the country.** You read the success stories of people like Henry Ford and Firestone -- well, those people started humbly. Henry Ford worked on the Model T in his own garage.

We look at these companies and think they have all the money and it's not fair. But if you go back to their origins, you'll find that many of them started lower than many of us. **Bill Gates is probably the richest man in America right now, yet he started with about $10,000 and without a college education**. Then there's Ted Turner. Everybody says Ted was born with a silver spoon in his mouth, but that's not true. If you read his story you'll find that Ted Turner was intensely motivated. He took big risks and some of them paid off big.

I remember once when Eileen and I were at a small floral shop in a very small town. I bought Eileen a plant and we were talking to the owner. She has a tiny store in a little tiny town. **Since we're all business people, I was bold enough to ask what they're grossing out of that store a year, and they told us they were grossing about $100,000 a year – out of a tiny store in a tiny town!** They're doing it by doing everything they can to serve that community. I think that's another important key to success.

That was certainly Sam Walton's secret. Sam Walton is kind of my personal hero. **Some people may think Sam got rich by ripping people off somehow, but if you read the book he wrote before he died, you'll see that the exact opposite is true: he made his great fortune by serving other people**. At one point in his book, Sam Walton said he had been in more K-Mart stores than any other person alive. He knew his business, and his competition, very well. He knew what they were doing wrong and set out to fix it -- and eventually K-mart had to adopt Sam's practices. **There aren't as many K-Marts around as there used to be, but when you go into one you're greeted with "Hi! How are you? Can we help you with something?"** They never used to do that years ago. But Sam Walton showed that greeters helped make the huge store more user-friendly. K-Mart and Target and all of the others have now followed his lead on that.

Wal-Mart does one thing that's really neat that most stores wouldn't do: their check-out machine does the check-writing for you. All you have to do is sign your name. It's just another service; they're always looking for ways to serve their customers better and they're willing to listen to suggestions from all venues. **Wal-Mart's greeter idea came from one of their local managers.** Lots of times you get your best ideas from just being in business, by serving your customers.

Everybody wants to know how to find that million dollar idea. **Well, the truth is, those million dollar ideas come from you as a process of doing business, serving your customers' needs, figuring out all the ways to help people.** This is the secret to making money in any business: think about how you can serve people better. What do they need? Look at every aspect of a person's life, especially the target market you're interested in, and ask, "What would people prefer to have? What enhancements to the product can I give them? What services can I provide? What books can I provide?" **Within your target area, think about how to make things better so you'll serve more people.**

When we first started M.O.R.E. Inc., in 1988, we were buying all different kinds of moneymaking books. We were desperately looking for a way to make more money and we were trying all sorts of new things. **By the time we finally found something that worked, we realized that most of those plans out there don't work.** So we had a good, strong knowledge of what people wanted and we wanted to really help people. It was something that we loved to do. The business we got started in was a natural extension of that.

Let's take a look at the assets you need in order to have a truly successful business. **While there are dozens of possibilities out there, four of them captivate me the most and I think they're vitally important:**

1. You have to have a combination of desire, persistence, and determination. Don't go into business unless you're gung-ho, really believe in yourself, and you really have that that desire, persistence, and determination in you. You'll need them when the going gets tough.

2. You need a target market. You don't want the whole world to be your customer, that's too hard to deal with. You want a specific target market.

3. You want to develop a product or service that will appeal to that target market, something that you can stand behind and feel good about.

4. You need a good copywriter. The marketing and promotion of your product is extraordinarily important.

Being in business presents many challenges. In fact, because of all the challenges, Eileen and I call it an exhilarated lifestyle. **Even things you perceive as a problem may really be opportunities in disguise.** Business is an exhilarated lifestyle because you have to do more than the average person does. You have more decisions to make. You have to do more. You have to put in more time, more passion, more of your energy. When some people go to a job they do the same thing over and over and over again -- but you don't do that when you run a business.

How can that be freedom? How can you be free and go to the same job and just do the same thing over and over again? Boring. Boring. Boring. There's nothing like that in our business. **When we got into this exciting direct response business we had to wear many hats and we never got bored. The same is still true.** Usually we have good days; sometimes we have bad days, but they're always exciting. We always know the potential for great success exists because we have the desire and determination we need. We're just going to do it because there's nobody else to do it for us. Remember that.

My biggest problem is that I get overwhelmed by things. **For example, I have five different projects to do today. When I first think about it as a whole, I get overwhelmed, but then when I think of the details instead of the projects as a whole, it all gets really simplified.** Business is a great way to build your self-confidence and your self-image. You're presented with new challenges all the time and you have to rise to them. You see people who have been in business a long time and they have that look about them; you think they're somehow different than you are. **But if someone has been in business for twenty years, like we have, they've already gone through a lot of problems**. Russ, who's been in the business 15 years longer, has already gone through the problems that we've gone through. When you work your way through the hard stuff, you develop more confidence and knowledge and experience and skills.

So don't let the problems and obstacles get you down. I know that that sounds so simplistic, but it's true -- you can just sail through your greatest problems in life. **You can go over them, under them, around them. Don't let those problems stop you.** I'm guilty of worrying, too, so I know how most people feel in a business situation. But the things we worry about seldom happen to us the way we think they will. Then, when sometimes we or a loved one does have a problem, it comes like a thief in the night.

We need to realize that we can do almost anything we want if we just stay focused and believe in ourselves. We're out there to serve people and to do a good job with products and services that people can use and really want. **I think it's important for you to remember that just getting started is the hardest part.** It's a popular analogy that people who have already made a million dollars and then somehow lost it can make that second million so much easier -- often in a tenth of the time it took them to make the first million. Then, if the bottom drops out, they could make their third million in a fraction of the time. It's just because they've developed the skills they need.

So don't give up: having the desire to succeed is the most important part of building a million dollar business. You really have to want the things I've talked about -- the tangible things like having a lot of money and the intangible things like being your own boss and not having somebody standing over your shoulder all the time. Think about when you were a little child, learning how to walk. **You wanted to walk so badly that it didn't matter how many times you fell down, how many times you hit your nose on the couch, or whatever.** You learned how to get up there and stand on your own two feet -- and you did it.

In the same way you can build a million dollar business. All you have to do is put the ideas I've talked about here into action and never stop trying!

www.ingramcontent.com/pod-product-compliance
Lightning Source LLC
LaVergne TN
LVHW050946080826
845145LV00004B/1428

* 9 7 8 1 9 3 3 3 5 6 0 2 0 *